White-Nosed Coati Raccoon's Cousin

by Joyce Markovics

Consultant: Christine Hass PhD
Biologist and Coati Expert

New York, New York

Credits

Cover and Title Page, © James Hager/Robert Harding Picture Library/SuperStock; 4L, © Douglas & Laurie W. Moore; 4R, © Joe Fuhrman; 5, © CarverMostardi/Alamy; 6T, © age fotostock/SuperStock; 6B, © Millard H Sharp/Photo Researchers/Getty Images; 7, © Alan Dahl/FocusedOnNature.com; 8T, © David Kuhn/Dwight Kuhn Photography; 8B, © Cubo Images/SuperStock; 9L, © Cynthia Kidwell/Shutterstock; 9R, © Luis César Tejo/Shutterstock; 10, © Photri Images/SuperStock; 11, © Cameron & Shirley Laing; 12, © Daniel Heuclin/NHPA/Photoshot; 13, © Max Waugh; 14, © Stan Tekiela/Nature Smart Images; 15, © Robin Chittenden/Alamy; 16, © Terry R. Steele; 17, © Stan Tekiela/Nature Smart Images; 18, © Max Waugh; 19, © Dick Dionne; 20, © Alan Dahl/FocusedOnNature.com; 21, © Paul Sutherland/National Geographic Stock; 22, © Robert Shantz/Alamy; 23, © AP Photo/Richard Richtmyer; 24, © DeepDesertPhoto/depositphotos/Pixmac; 25, © Dick Dionne; 26-27, © imagebroker/SuperStock; 28, © Robert Shantz/Alamy; 29, Courtesy of arcforwildlife.com.

Publisher: Kenn Goin
Senior Editor: Lisa Wiseman
Creative Director: Spencer Brinker
Design: Dawn Beard Creative
Photo Researcher: Daniella Nilva

Library of Congress Cataloging-in-Publication Data

Markovics, Joyce L.
 White-nosed coati : raccoon's cousin / by Joyce Markovics.
    p. cm. — (America's hidden animal treasures)
 Includes bibliographical references and index.
 ISBN 978-1-61772-581-4 (library binding) — ISBN 1-61772-581-1 (library binding)
1. Coatis—Juvenile literature. I. Title.
 QL737.C26M375 2013
 599.76'3—dc23
                                    2012016961

For more information, write to Bearport Publishing Company, Inc., 45 West 21st Street, Suite 3B, New York, New York 10010. Printed in the United States of America in North Mankato, Minnesota.

10 9 8 7 6 5 4 3 2 1

Contents

"A Monkey in Madera Canyon"

One sunny morning in late summer, **naturalist** Doug Moore was driving in Madera Canyon in southeastern Arizona. Suddenly, he noticed a strange-looking animal in the middle of the road. Doug slowed down and peered through the windshield. As the car inched closer, the animal spun around to face the car head-on!

Madera Canyon is a large wilderness area that attracts many hikers and visitors each year.

Doug Moore teaches classes about nature at Madera Canyon.

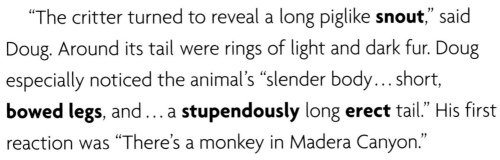

"The critter turned to reveal a long piglike **snout**," said Doug. Around its tail were rings of light and dark fur. Doug especially noticed the animal's "slender body…short, **bowed legs**, and…a **stupendously** long **erect** tail." His first reaction was "There's a monkey in Madera Canyon."

Doug stopped his car and was able to get a good look at the animal. He soon realized that it was not a monkey at all. It was a white-nosed coati (koh-AH-tee), one of America's hidden animal treasures.

There are three known types of coatis: white-nosed coatis (shown here), South American coatis, and mountain coatis.

The white-nosed coati gets its name from the patch of white fur on its snout.

Raccoon Relative

White-nosed coatis are small **mammals** found in the Southwest United States, Mexico, and Central America. They may also live in northern parts of Colombia in South America. Because coatis are **rare** and not often seen by people, they are often mistaken for other animals, such as raccoons. In fact, coatis and raccoons are closely related and similar in many ways. For example, both animals have black fur on their faces and a furry, ringed tail. Also, like their raccoon cousins, coatis are very intelligent.

A full-grown coati (top) weighs anywhere from 8 to 16 pounds (4 to 7 kg)—about the size of an adult raccoon (bottom).

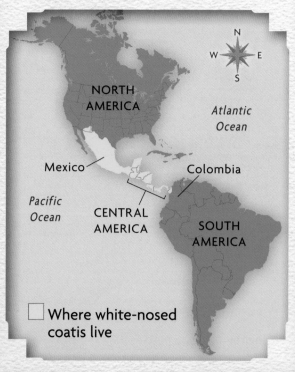

White-Nosed Coatis in the Wild

NORTH AMERICA

Atlantic Ocean

Mexico

Colombia

Pacific Ocean

CENTRAL AMERICA

SOUTH AMERICA

☐ Where white-nosed coatis live

Even though coatis and raccoons are related, they're not exactly alike. For example, a coati's tail is much longer than a raccoon's, which may be up to 12 inches (30 cm) long. A coati's tail can be up to 27 inches (69 cm) in length—that's more than half the length of its body! Another difference is that coatis are active during the daytime, which is when raccoons are usually asleep.

The white-nosed coati has an extremely long tail.

Coatis live in woodlands or in canyons, where good water sources are located.

Food Time

During the day, coatis spend most of their time searching for food. As they ramble along, they use their bearlike paws and long, sensitive snouts to explore sand and soil or to push dead leaves out of the way. The tip of a coati's nose is very flexible and can be used to quickly uncover a delicious snack buried deep in the ground.

Coatis spend about 90 percent of each day looking for food.

Coatis love to eat the fruit that grows on the prickly pear cactus.

Coatis will eat anything from insects to eggs to fruit. They are not picky. Their long, curved claws are well suited for digging up earthworms. Once the worms are dug up, the coatis use their sharp teeth to pick them out of the soil. Coatis also use their lightning-quick front paws to catch small animals, such as mice, lizards, and frogs, which they kill with a bite to the head.

A coati uses its sharp claws and teeth to help it catch prey.

A Taste for Tarantulas

Among the coatis' favorite snacks are tarantulas! However, these huge spiders are not an easy meal to eat. Why? Their bodies are covered with prickly hairs that can **irritate** a coati when they become stuck in the animal's eyes, nose, and throat. So coatis have come up with a clever technique for removing these hairs before eating the spiders.

Tarantulas are large, hairy spiders that are found mainly in warm climates.

If they are threatened, tarantulas can flick the irritating hairs from their bodies at their attackers.

After capturing a tarantula with its front paws, a coati forcefully rolls the spider around in the dirt. This "dirt bath" causes the spider's hairs to fall out so that the coati can safely devour it.

A coati rolling a tarantula in the dirt

All in a Day's Work

To find food, such as tarantulas, coatis may walk up to 1.5 miles (2.4 m) a day. As they wander, they search for food not only on the ground but also high up in trees. In fact, coatis spend about half their time in trees. According to zookeeper Jeanne Minor, "Coatis are graceful climbers. They look as much at home up in trees as they do on the ground."

A coati can easily and quickly climb up and down trees.

Coatis can **rotate** their ankles so that their back feet face sideways. This allows them to hold onto the tree trunk as they slide down headfirst.

When they're not crawling up tree trunks and along branches to find food, coatis can be found in trees for other reasons. They often take naps on branches or use trees as places to escape from **predators**, such as jaguars and other large wildcats. Coatis use their long tails to help them balance as they dart up and down trees and across narrow branches. Scientists have watched them climb as high as 98 feet (30 m)—that's as high as a nine-story building!

Coatis often rest in treetops when it's hot out, because it's cool in the shade of the tree branches.

Living in a Troop

Coatis are often spotted exploring treetops with other coatis. That is because they live in large groups called **troops**, consisting of 12 to 30 animals. Most members of a troop, which is made up of females and young males, are related. The females are in charge of the group. Adult male coatis generally live alone.

When coatis walk together, they sometimes hold their tails straight up in the air like exclamation points. This helps them keep track of each other in tall grass.

This troop of coatis is looking for food. Staying in a large group helps coatis stay safe from predators.

Once a year, however, adult male and female coatis come together to **mate**. About 11 weeks after they've mated, the females are ready to give birth. To prepare for their young, the females separate from their troop. Then each one builds a nest high up in a tree. There, the babies will be protected from predators on the ground, such as jaguars, pumas, and large snakes.

Male coatis are about twice as big as females. They start living on their own after two years of age.

Raising a Family

A mother coati usually has a **litter** of two to seven babies. The young coatis are ready to leave the tree nest when they are five weeks old. At that time, the mother coati and her babies rejoin the troop. The females within a particular troop work together to help raise each other's babies, even if they are not related. The babies are **groomed**, **nursed**, and cared for by all the females.

Baby coatis look like miniature adults.

Coati babies weigh 3.5 to 6.3 ounces (99 to 179 g) when they are born. That's about the weight of four slices of bread.

Female coatis use their paws and long claws to groom the babies—and each other. They remove harmful bugs, such as ticks, from the skin and fur. Grooming also helps young and old coatis maintain a close relationship.

Here, an adult coati and a young coati search for a meal.

Girl Power

Female coatis also work together to protect their **offspring**. While **foraging** for food, females will position themselves so that their young are kept in the center of the group. This keeps them safe from a predator's attack.

White-nosed coatis foraging for food on a beach

As they're searching for food, coatis use many types of sounds to communicate with each other. For example, they make a grunting sound to maintain contact with other coatis in their troop. Also, when a female feels **threatened** or notices a predator, she will bark and twitch her tail to warn others to be on the lookout.

Coatis that feel threatened will sometimes bare their teeth and lower their heads, much like dogs.

Clowning Around

The females continue to watch over the young coatis for several months. During this time, the young animals spend a lot of time playing. "Youngsters play very frequently," said **biologist** Christine Hass, who has studied coatis in the wild. "They use their front legs to bat at each other." The playful coatis also wrestle, roll around, and chase each other across the forest floor. "I have seen entire troops chasing each other up and around dead trees," said Christine.

Two young coatis playfully trying to get food out of a bird feeder

As a result of their playful and curious nature, coatis have been known to get into trouble. At the National Zoo in Washington, D.C., the white-nosed coatis climbed the walls of their pen and learned how to unscrew lamps and lightbulbs from the ceiling. The coatis then used the lightbulbs and metal screws they collected as toys!

A coati living at the National Zoo in Washington, D.C.

When coatis are playing, they sometimes stand on their back legs and spread their front legs, as if they are about to hug one another. They also open their mouths, as if they are grinning.

Threats

Few people in the United States ever get a chance to see white-nosed coatis playing in the wild. That's because coatis are rare in the United States. According to Christine Hass, there may be fewer than 4,000 living in the United States today.

Very few people in the United States ever get to see a white-nosed coati.

One reason for such a small coati population is that people sometimes hunt them. In some areas, coatis may be hunted for their meat or for **sport**. Coatis are also accidentally killed in traps set by hunters looking to catch other animals. In addition, coatis are sometimes killed by mistake when they eat poison that people put out for other animals, such as coyotes.

Even though coatis face several different threats, people are doing many things to help them. In some places, such as New Mexico, the government has passed laws that protect coatis from being hunted or trapped.

Coatis live for 5 to 10 years in the wild and up to 20 years in **captivity**.

White-nosed coatis in captivity

Disappearing Homes

While laws like the ones in New Mexico help coatis, the animals are still not safe. They have an even bigger problem to deal with: **habitat** loss. As humans **pollute** rivers and streams and cut down forests to make room for homes and businesses, coatis are forced to find new places to live. Sometimes, these places are very **isolated**, with no other coatis around, except those within the same family group.

"The biggest threats to coatis in the United States are probably habitat loss and hunting," said Christine Hass.

Coatis living in isolated habitats are forced to breed with each other. Over time, this **inbreeding** can harm the health of coatis and make them get sick more easily. It can also eventually lead to death, which further reduces the number of coatis in the United States.

Coatis living in the United States may eventually die out if they are unable to find other healthy coatis to breed with.

Deadly diseases carried by other animals also threaten coatis. For example, coatis can get **canine distemper** from dogs and **rabies** from skunks or foxes.

Coatis for Sale

Experts are also concerned about another problem facing white-nosed coatis: they are being sold as pets. In some states, it is legal to keep coatis as household pets. Although some coatis easily **adapt** to being around people, they can cause a lot of trouble inside human homes.

Some people who sell coatis as pets remove their teeth and claws so that the animals can't bite or scratch.

Despite their cute appearance, coatis are wild animals that are difficult to handle. They love to climb and can easily get into cabinets and destroy furniture. The best place for these amazing animals is in their natural habitat, where they can live and play freely.

In some areas of Central and South America, wild coatis and people live side by side.

White-Nosed Coati Facts

The scientific name for a white-nosed coati is *Nasua narica*. A coati has a long body and a slender head. It uses its exceptionally long, piglike nose to sniff out food. Here are some more facts about this animal.

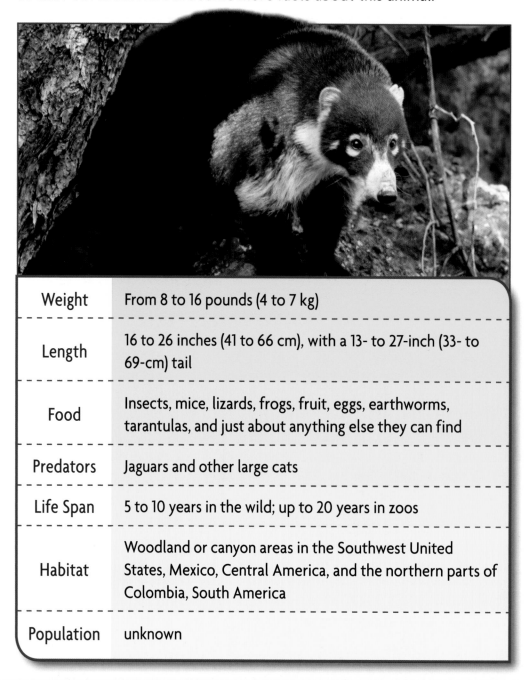

Weight	From 8 to 16 pounds (4 to 7 kg)
Length	16 to 26 inches (41 to 66 cm), with a 13- to 27-inch (33- to 69-cm) tail
Food	Insects, mice, lizards, frogs, fruit, eggs, earthworms, tarantulas, and just about anything else they can find
Predators	Jaguars and other large cats
Life Span	5 to 10 years in the wild; up to 20 years in zoos
Habitat	Woodland or canyon areas in the Southwest United States, Mexico, Central America, and the northern parts of Colombia, South America
Population	unknown

People Helping Coatis

There are many threats facing coatis today, including habitat loss and hunting. Also, many coatis are bought as pets and then **abused** or **abandoned**. Luckily, there are groups that are working hard to save some coatis. Here are two of these organizations:

Arizona Coati Rescue and Education (A.C.R.E.)

- A.C.R.E. is dedicated to raising and caring for unwanted coatis that were bred as pets.
- Some people who sell coatis as pets remove the animals' teeth and claws. As a result, these coatis can no longer live on their own. A.C.R.E. cares for these animals by providing them with proper food and shelter.
- The organization also works to teach people about coatis' special needs and why they do not make good pets.

A rescued coati that was abused by its owner

Rainbow Wildlife Rescue

- Located outside Weatherford, Texas, Rainbow Wildlife Rescue saves and cares for wild coatis that have been injured, or abandoned coatis that were kept as pets.
- Rainbow Wildlife Rescue includes a two-story barn that houses its coatis and an outside area where the animals can run and play.
- The group's founder, Birgit Sommer, has been helping injured and orphaned wildlife since 2004. She also helps educate people about coatis and other local wildlife.

Glossary

abandoned (uh-BAN-duhnd) left alone, without help

abused (uh-BYOOSSD) treated badly or cruelly

adapt (uh-DAPT) to change over time

biologist (bye-OL-uh-jist) a scientist who studies animals or plants

bowed legs (BOHD LEGS) legs that are curved outward so that the knees don't touch when the ankles are together

canine distemper (KAY-nine diss-TEM-pur) an often deadly disease that affects some animals, causing fever and coughing

captivity (kap-TIV-uh-*tee*) a place where an animal lives that is not its natural home and where it cannot travel freely

erect (i-REKT) standing upright

foraging (FOR-ij-ing) looking for food in the wild

groomed (GROOMD) when the fur or skin of an animal is cleaned

habitat (HAB-uh-*tat*) a place in nature where an animal is normally found

inbreeding (IN-*breed*-ing) the mating of closely related individuals

irritate (IHR-uh-tate) to annoy or bother

isolated (EYE-suh-*late*-id) kept separate and away from others

litter (LIT-ur) a group of animals that are born to the same mother at the same time

mammals (MAM-uhlz) animals that are warm-blooded, nurse their young with milk, and have hair or fur on their skin

mate (MATE) to come together to have young

naturalist (NACH-ur-uhl-ist) a person who studies animals and plants

nursed (NURSST) fed a young animal with milk that comes from its mother

offspring (AWF-spring) an animal's young

pollute (puh-LOOT) to release harmful substances into the air, water, or soil

predators (PRED-uh-turz) animals that hunt other animals for food

rabies (RAY-beez) a deadly disease caused by a virus that attacks the brain and spinal cord and is spread by the bite of an infected animal

rare (RAIR) not often seen or found

rotate (ROH-tate) to turn around

snout (SNOUT) the long front part of an animal's head that sticks out; it includes the nose, and usually the jaws and mouth

sport (SPORT) something done for fun

stupendously (stoo-PEN-duhss-lee) amazingly or extremely

threatened (THRET-uhnd) being in immediate danger

troops (TROOPS) groups of animals that live and do things together

Bibliography

BBC, Nature Wildlife
(www.bbc.co.uk/nature/life/White-nosed_Coati)

Los Angeles Zoo & Botanic Gardens
(lazoo.org/animals/mammals/coati_whitenosed/index.html)

The Mammals of Texas, Online Edition
(www.nsrl.ttu.edu/tmot1/nasunari.htm)

Smithsonian National Zoological Park
(nationalzoo.si.edu/publications/zoogoer/1997/3/coatisatthezoo.cfm)

Read More

Parker, Steve. *Mammal.* New York: DK Children (2004).

Patent, Dorothy Hinshaw. *Life in a Desert.* Minneapolis, MN: Lerner Publishing Group (2003).

Read, Tracy C. *Exploring the World of Raccoons.* Buffalo, NY: Firefly Books (2010).

Learn More Online

To learn more about white-nosed coatis, visit
www.bearportpublishing.com/AmericasHiddenAnimalTreasures

Index

About the Author

Joyce Markovics is a writer and editor in New York City. She lives
with her husband, Adam, and a spirited rabbit named Pearl, that is
mischievous, just like coatis!